Thinning Edges:
A Chemical Reaction

Identify the Problem
and Transition to Natural Hair

Cathy Howse

© 2006 Thinning Edges: A Chemical Reaction—Identify the Problem and Transition to Natural Hair

UBH Publications Inc
PO Box 22678
Denver, CO 80222

Publishers Cataloging in Publication Data

Cathy Howse
    Thinning Edges: A Chemical Reaction–Identify the Problem
    and Transition to Natural Hair

ISBN   978-0-9785659-0-9

1. Black Hair Care   2. Natural Hair Care
3. Black Hair Growth   4. Chemical Relaxed Hair
5. Afro-American women hair   6. Hair-Care and Hygiene
7. Hairdressing of African Americans   8. Hair Straightening
9. Hair Care Tips and Tools   I. Cathy Howse
II. Title

www.ultrablackhair.com
Printed in the United States of America

FIRST EDITION

Dedicated to
Every Black woman who realizes
knowledge and truth about her hair is empowering

Acknowledgements
First and foremost, thank you Jehovah for this wisdom. I am grateful to
all of my customers for their contributions, encouragement and loyalty.
To the A'Lelia Bundles/Walker Family Collection for the use of Madam
Walker's picture. This book could not have been written without the
support of Lila Abrams and Linda Moore. Finally, I want to thank my
staff, family and friends who encouraged me and kept
me motivated.

Publisher's Note

This book is designed to provide information regarding the subject matter covered. It is sold with the understanding that neither the author nor publisher are engaged in rendering legal or professional advice, and the reader should seek legal or professional assistance if required.

The purpose of this book is to inform and suggest and not to advise or recommend. Therefore, the author nor publisher shall have neither liability nor responsibility to any person or entity with respect to any loss or damage caused or alleged to be caused, directly or indirectly, by the information contained in this book.

Every effort has been made to make this book as complete and accurate as possible. Neither author nor publisher are responsible for any information changed subsequent to the publishing of this book.

Neither financial interest nor compensation was received by the author or publisher for any mentions of any products or companies in Thinning Edges: A Chemical Reaction–Identify the Problem and Transition to Natural Hair.

Introduction

This book will help you understand your unique Black hair care issues, especially as they relate to thinning edges. These issues touch our hearts and souls because we live them–and I for one know we can no longer just commiserate about them, we must do something about them.

This book establishes guidelines to help you create a system to prevent thinning edges and maintain your beautiful Black hair. Its approach is twofold. It addresses both the damage chemical relaxers can do to Black hair and offers real solutions and guidelines for maintaining healthy, beautiful NATURAL hair.

This book provides instruction for safe use and application of chemical relaxers. If you have made the decision to go au naturel it provides instruction on how to keep and grow the hair you have while you make the transition.

This book is the first step to taking control of your hair!

Table of Contents

Madam C.J. Walker, Hair Care Entrepreneur
1867-1919

1. In the Beginning
a hairstory of Black hair

Nothing new about Black women and hair loss

The problem of thinning Black hair has manifest over the years and remains a critical issue for Black women. Sarah Breedlove McWilliams Walker, better known as Madam C. J. Walker dealt with it back in the early 1900s. A pioneer in the hair care world, she experimented with a variety of homemade remedies in hopes of eliminating many of the hair issues confronting Black women as well as her own hair loss problems and scalp ailments. Soon Madam Walker's Wonderful Hair Grower, a scalp conditioning and healing formula was born. Her scalp conditioners, shampoos and hair ointments were popular and made her one of America's first Black millionaires. "Because most American women lacked indoor plumbing, central heating and electricity, hygiene practices were quite different in Madam Walker's day. Her revolutionary system, which encouraged women to wash their hair more often and to apply a sulfur-based ointment, healed the scalp disease that was so rampant a century ago," according to Walker's great-great-granddaughter and biographer, A'Lelia Bundles.

Really poor hair care and infrequent hair washing caused most of our hair problems back then. And though Madam Walker's products worked to maintain already healthy hair, we continue to have hair issues, most of which have nothing to do with clean hair. In many cases, the hair damage we experience today results from the use and misapplication of chemicals on our scalps.

What are industry innovators and experts doing about it?

The industry wants us to believe we have to put something on our scalps to have beautiful hair. Not a great challenge considering we grow up putting things on our scalps; after all, it is a part of our culture. But why? No other race does. We are the only people who put things on our scalps to supposedly maintain healthy hair. So between the industry and our upbringing we end up victims of our own hair care experiments and cultural beliefs. But what choice do we have? No one else is doing anything about it. No one in the industry is researching why our hair is falling out or why our edges are thinning or why we do not produce long hair without continuous and constant care. So we experiment, turning our kitchens and bathrooms into science labs and destroying our hair.

The industry loves the fact Black women have thinning edges and balding heads because they are in the business of of selling hair—and selling weave and wigs is far more profitable than product research and development. Industry experts realized long ago the profit margins in female hair care products. Have you been in a hair supply store lately? It is overwhelming how many types, pieces and styles of hair are available on the market, an ever-growing market I might add. But this is no surprise to industry analysts. They knew fake hair would be profitable because there was no real focus on female hair loss prevention despite the millions of women facing hair loss due to genetics, stress, scalp disease, illness, drugs or childbirth. Increase the numbers for Black women because hair loss due to the conditions above as well as the misuse of chemical products. So instead of solutions to keep our natural hair, they solved our problems with fake hair—which we purchase happily and willingly and affix atop our heads because we do not believe we have any other choice.

Do not buy into the hair hype! Do not let your hair obsession keep you from taking care of your own hair. Your lack of concern and care for your hair is what the industry wants and expects; it is what makes them rich. Do not get me wrong; I am not telling you to avoid getting your "hair on." I just want to reinforce through this book the importance of having a healthy head of hair beneath that wig or weave as well as offer some steps that can help get you there!

I thought nothing of my hair thinning

I had never noticed thinning hair on Black women until I spent time at industry tradeshows. In fact, it was just after attending a tradeshow when I became aware of my own thinning hair. I had pulled my hair back exposing two short sections of hair on each of my temples when my sister asked if I was experiencing breakage. I had noticed shorter hair in these spots but thought nothing of them. After that day, I began to pay closer attention to those sparse areas on my head and did all the moisturizing and care I thought was required to repair them. Unfortunately, these areas just stayed the same, shorter than all the other hair around them. It did not take long before I realized what was causing my thinning hair—the use of chemical products. Also, I began wondering if my next retouch would permanently remove all my hair!

It did not take long to face reality. I knew even if I took the greatest care applying my relaxer retouches some of the chemical would inevitably get on my scalp. I tried to convince myself differently but I kept thinking about how the prolonged use of chemicals could and eventually would cause irreversible damage to my hair follicles which would result in baldness. So I stopped using chemical relaxers on my head altogether.

All of my research involved hair breakage

As a result of my own thinning hair issues, I felt compelled to investigate the problem. Yet, I knew absolutely nothing about it because all of my research had dealt with hair breakage. Adding to my concern was the number of emails I began to receive related to thinning hair. The more emails I received the more painfully aware I became of the prevalence of Black women with thinning hair issues. So I decided to do some research on the topic. What causes the problem and why? Unfortunately, a lot of what I discovered did not make good practice and provided no real solutions.

To adequately approach a solution for the problem of thinning edges, I would have to go back to where the problem began—in the kitchens and bathrooms of Black women—the two rooms we use to rectify our hair issues and mishaps. This is why we are known as "kitchen beauticians" and the originators of the hair care experiment. We experiment on our own hair, on our daughter's hair and anyone else who is willing to take a spin in the "kitchen beautician's" chair. But what happens when the experiment fails? What happens when the hair falls out or massive burning occurs? Who do we call? Who are we going to ask about our failed experiment?

We keep our fingers crossed and hope for the best

You can ask your hairdresser, but you are unlikely to get a solid answer. Yes, there are plenty of knowledgeable hairdressers out there. There are also plenty of hairdressers as perplexed as we are—hairdressers who ridicule our questions or give us impractical or misinformation as a result of their own lack of knowledge. Therefore, with no where to turn, we just accept our thinning edges and hope some day our missing hair will return.

So we keep our fingers crossed as we continue to apply things to our scalps because our culture and the hair care industry say we should do so if we want to have beautiful hair. And we do this despite the years of proof that doing so does not work. We have been convinced that our real problem is excessively dry hair and the remedy must be applied directly to our scalps. It does not matter if your remedy is hair oil or chemical relaxer; one of them will be the answer to our hair woes or that is what we are led to believe.

However, putting things on our scalps does not relieve anything and is actually the real cause of many of our hair issues. And of all the things we do apply, the biggest culprit of thinning edges and bald spots is chemical relaxer, which is pressed into our scalp to make the hair as straight as possible. Unfortunately, the result is not straighter hair but hair loss. Putting a chemical relaxer on the scalp acts much in the same way a nicotine patch would, releasing the medicine into the skin, or in this case, chemicals into the scalp. Just like skin, a scalp has pores. We subject our pores to relaxer chemicals for up to 30 minutes eight times a year, more than enough time to penetrate the scalp and cause permanent hair loss.

I loved my relaxed hair

I am not bashing relaxers. I would love to have my hair straightened permanently. However, I realized having relaxed hair could result in serious consequences, and I made the choice not to take the chance. Keeping my hair healthy and beautiful is my goal and the goal of many Black women. Yet, for others, it is a dream deferred. I have witnessed the embarrassment, shame and devastation some Black women face when they realize their hair is gone forever and they may have to rely on wigs and weaves for the rest of their lives. It is sad to see so many thinning hair edges and sides as well as bald spots, but no one wants to admit that a multi-million dollar industry might be the leading cause of our missing hair. We do not want to give up the tried and true—which are our wigs, weaves and straight hair. Yet, we may not have a choice.

So what do we do now?

I know you are thinking, is this my only alternative? I know you are wondering if you choose to go au naturel will you have to cut off your relaxed hair or will you still be able to straighten your hair. And finally, I know you are wondering what the transition back to natural hair process involves?

First, making the decision to go natural will not mean you have to cut off your processed hair. It does mean you will need to be committed to the transition process if you are serious about keeping your hair on your head. And this book, *Thinning Edges: A Chemical Reaction,* is the hair care manual to help you through the transitioning process, whether you continue to use chemicals or not.

It is sad and embarrassing to see thin hair edges and sides on so many Black women. It is happening too much to ignore, and I know the only way to prevent total balding is to stop chemically relaxing our hair!

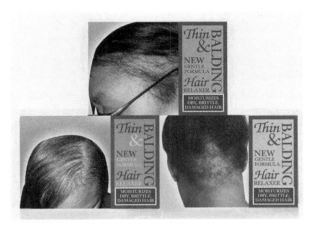

2. Chemical Relaxers
how safe are they?

The real reason for our hair loss

Why is the pattern of thinning hair so prevalent amongst Black women? Why is it happening when neither our mothers nor grandmothers experienced thinning hair or bald spots?

Visiting Black expos and tradeshows gave me all the evidence I needed to come to this conclusion, something has gone dramatically wrong with our hair. I saw Black woman after Black woman with missing sides, bald patches in the front, hairlines back to their ears and braids attached to tiny pieces of hair. Others wore braids where the hair was so sparse the braids were spread an inch apart. Some hid their thinning and balding under weaves and wigs, while others managed to sport what little hair they had. I saw young women and older women and every age in between. It was sad to see women in their 20's who should have beautiful, healthy hair but instead had balding, thinning hair—hair that barely reached their ears—hair that had fallen out in patches—hair that just would not grow past their earlobes let alone their shoulders.

Types of hair loss

Severe hair loss can be devastating. One day you have hair, the next day you do not. Even the smallest bare spot, no matter how well concealed, can affect your self esteem because you know it is there—and you think others know it is there too! Millions of people suffer from hair loss, but few understand why or what type of hair loss condition they have. According to *Milay's Standard Textbook of Cosmetology*, hair scientists have defined 5 types of hair loss:

- **Androgenetic Alopecia** — is defined as the most common type of hair loss type; it starts during teen years and is hereditary. It is affected by hormones and age. In men, it is most commonly referred to as male pattern baldness. However, women are subject to this condition as well.

- **Alopecia Areata** — is defined as sudden hair loss and is most often attributed to stress. Characteristics include round or irregular patches of hair loss.

- **Telogen Effluvium** — is defined as hair that sheds prematurely for various reasons, including childbirth, birth control pills, crash diets, fever, shock or drug intake.

- **Traction or Traumatic Alopecia** — is defined as a traumatic condition caused by repetitive pulling of the hair (braids) and has been attributed to excessive chemical applications or excessive pressing comb use.

- **Postpartum Alopecia** — is defined as a temporary hair loss condition after pregnancy and is affected by hormone levels in the body.

Many of the reasons for hair loss cannot be helped while others are very preventable. For Black women, much of our thinning hair issues can be resolved by the elimination of chemicals on our hair. But we do love our straight hair; yet for most of us to achieve straight hair we believe we must apply a chemical relaxer. At least, this is just the notion the hair care industry wants you to have because this is the notion that helps them sell products.

In 2000, around 75% of adult Black women relaxed their hair, which translated into more than $200 million for the manufacturers of relaxers and associated products. "Perm and relaxer sales were down to $99 million in 2005, but industry analysts expect sales to double over the next 2 years." And knowing how much we love our straight hair as well as the ongoing trend toward long, straight hair, doubling their sales should not be a great challenge. Now, there is nothing wrong with wanting to have straight hair, but there is something wrong when getting it results in hair loss!

The misapplication of chemical relaxers

Over the years, we have tried to find solutions to our hair concerns, and based on emails I receive from individuals who have sought professional advice, it appears the recommendations run the gamut and are ascribed a variety of causes. One of the causes is one of the 5 defined hair loss types, Traumatic Alopecia—meaning the hair was not predestined to fall out something made it fall out. Could that something be applying a chemical relaxer? Of course, it could!

If you use chemical relaxers and your hair falls off your head within hours or days after a retouch, it should be considered a reaction to a very caustic chemical. What else could it be? It is obvious what caused your hair loss. Even if you experience gradual hair density loss, you can bet it is happening because your scalp can no longer handle the relaxer and has permitted the relaxer chemicals to disable your hair cells.

Can you relate? What do see in the mirror? Is it a ½" to 1" of hair that never grows any longer while all the other hair around it seems to flourish? Do you have baby hair (peach fuzz) that appears not to grow? Fact is, it is growing in, but it is falling out just as quickly because scalp damaging chemicals have changed or permanently altered the cellular structure of the hair beneath the scalp.

Why are you putting hair removal chemicals on your hair?

When we relax our hair we are using a chemical with a pH the equivalency of crème depilatories—yeah, the same stuff you use to remove hair from legs! Meaning each time you relax your hair, you run the risk of removing your hair from your head and causing damage that ranges from severe burns to permanent scalp damage. So if you choose to use a chemical relaxer, contact with the scalp must be avoided because relaxer repeatedly pushed onto the scalp will eventually cause hair loss at the follicle site where the scalp has been burned. I realize it is nearly impossible to apply a relaxer without getting some on your scalp, so I offer some tips on how to apply relaxer in the next chapter. Well, that is if the next few paragraphs do not scare you into keeping chemical relaxers off your head altogether.

Relaxers contain drain cleaner

Yes, drain cleaner! The pH of "Lye" used to unclog your drain is greater than 12. Chemical relaxer pH is between 10 and 13.5, whereas pure lye has a pH of 14. Relaxers feature very powerful chemicals. And just think about this, not only do you put relaxer on your heads but you allow it to run all over your bodies when we rinse out the relaxer from our hair in the shower. You would not spread perm or relaxer over your body and leave it on for even 5

You would not spread perm or relaxer over your body and leave it on for even 5 minutes because you know 3rd degree chemical burns would result. So how do you justify putting it on your head even longer?

minutes because you know 3rd degree chemical burns could result. So how do you justify putting it on your head for that long and even longer? If you plan to continue using relaxers think twice about rinsing out your hair in the shower and use a sink instead.

Lye or "no lye", the results are the same

Now if you are not worried about using chemical relaxers because you use a no lye relaxer, then do not get too comfortable with that lack of concern. If you look at the ingredients on the relaxer box, it lists sodium hydroxide—real name lye. The main ingredient on the no lye relaxer box is either calcium hydroxide, guanidine hydroxide or potassium hydroxide; do not be fooled, under any of those names it is still lye. It just contains lower pH levels and supposedly relaxes more slowly so "kitchen beauticians" do not have to hurry to get it on before the hair starts straightening or the scalp starts burning.

Yes, I know. Why did I have to go and remove the one fact that brought you comfort and made you feel safe about relaxing your hair. I had no choice, you are putting liquid drain cleaner on your head. If you look up "lye" in the dictionary, it says: 2) see potassium hydroxide 3) see sodium hydroxide, which is defined as "a caustic white solid used as a bleach and in the manufacture of batteries." Now that is just plain scary. Manufacturers should be ashamed of themselves hiding something so dangerous under those scientific names; they should just come out and say what it is!

No lye relaxers are still lye just by another name

Do not let clever marketing techniques fool you!

We can no longer try to convince ourselves chemical relaxers are okay to use on our heads. Do not let the industry pull the wool over your eyes by buying into clever marketing techniques designed to have you believe their safe. Hair care entrepreneur, George H. Johnson, learned that clever marketing strategies can make you rich, but they can make you poor too. In 1954, he developed a "safe" permanent straightening system which could be purchased for use in the home. So Black women purchased the straightening system because they wanted straight hair, but their decision to buy was reinforced by that word "safe." So they gave no real thought to what was really being offered to them. In 1964, the hair care industry noticed Johnson was making millions off his invention and others wanted to capitalize on his success. The notoriety forced Johnson to disclose that his "safe" permanent straightening system contained lye! And though all the other relaxer brands on the market then contained lye too, he was the only manufacturer subject to disclosure for nearly 2 years. Needless to say, the public scrutiny and customer distrust cost Johnson his market share.

The title to this chapter is: *Chemical relaxers, how safe are they?* Well, having read this far how would you answer that question? I realize some of you will not be concerned enough by what you have read to stop using chemical relaxers. So the next chapter will give you safe methods for relaxer use and application. However, if this chapter scared you right out of the relaxer aisle, then Chapter 4 will give you the steps you need to transition back to your natural hair.

Summary

Alopecia basically means hair loss.

Traumatic alopecia results from relaxer use and is preventable.

Cleaver marketing implies relaxers are safe. *They are only safe when they do not come in contact with the scalp.*

Relaxer chemicals are equivalent to *putting liquid drain cleaner on your head.*

All relaxers cause breaking and thinning if they are repeatedly pushed onto the scalp.

Relaxers, perms, and hair dye are chemicals and will *all result in thinning hair if they are improperly applied.*

Lye or no lye, it makes no difference where relaxers are concerned.

3. Have Great Relaxed Hair
proper technique and application

Have straightened hair, but safely

The decision to give up your relaxed hair can be a tough one, especially if it means changing your hairstyle or daily routine. Some of you may decide relaxed hair is convenient and is your look of choice, and therefore will continue to use chemical relaxers in your hair. If this is you, then this chapter offers proper techniques and application processes for use of chemical relaxer.

Many hairdressers apply relaxer using the back of their hand or the back of the comb, pushing the product close to or on to the scalp. This is not a good technique and will eventually damage your hair and harm your scalp. Think about it, you get a retouch regularly every 6 to 8 weeks. If your hairdresser is using the wrong technique this will result in hair loss every 6 to 8 weeks—you can bet on it!

There is no doubt the use of chemical relaxer, if applied correctly, will straighten afro-textured hair successfully and keep hair loss to a minimum. The cosmetology textbooks explain exactly how to apply a relaxer and hairdressers apply relaxers exactly according to professional class instructions and textbooks. But something is going wrong in the application process and it is causing major hair loss. It is the practice of improper procedure which has hairdressers as well as self applicants pushing relaxer into the scalp at great risk to the health of the hair follicle. I believe it is the relaxer smoothing technique causing Black women to go bald—the process recommended to hairdressers and self applicants by hair care professionals in the industry textbooks and courses.

Faulty Instructions

The *Textbook of Cosmetology* offers three methods for applying a chemical relaxer to the hair: *comb method, color applicator brush or finger method.* After the relaxer is applied, the smoothing process is initiated. It is important because as the hair softens from the chemical the manual smoothing process helps make the hair straighter and straighter when applied using one of the methods mentioned above. However, the industry publication used to train beauty school students fails to offer adequate instructions on how to smooth the relaxer in a manner less damaging to the scalp. An improper smoothing procedure can result in thinning and balding problems, and unfortunately the industry textbook teaches a *faulty smoothing technique.*

The cosmetology training manual instructs students to use fingers and palms as well as the back of a comb for chemical application. Be wary of this advice! Using the palms and fingers to manipulate the chemical treatment invites contact with the scalp, and this is exactly what you do not want.

The textbook cautions the user to wear protective gloves to prevent damage to your hands, but it fails to acknowledge possible damage to the scalp by using this palms and fingers smoothing technique. This lack of information from industry teaching professionals and textbook publishers is partially responsible for the improper use of these products. The very textbook used to obtain licensing recommends smoothing the chemical against the scalp and provides inadequate to non-existent caution against potential damage. They should be held accountable by Black women whose relaxed hair is falling right off of their heads as a result.

Keep relaxer off your scalp

So the goal is to keep relaxers off the scalp, but you cannot do that if the chemical is deliberately pushed onto it. Many books attempt to guide you through relaxer applications; this is where you have to be cautious, even if the photographs show relaxer applied all the way to the scalp. I performed my own relaxer retouches for years.

It is mission critical to keep relaxers off your scalp

Sometimes I would have a friend apply them, and other times I would go to the salon. It is hard to tell a hairdresser to keep the product off the scalp because they have their professional technique and see themselves as the expert, as it should be. After all, they are trained to apply relaxer, but you are the one who will suffer if the relaxer application goes bad! Maybe it is just me, but I will not allow any one to damage my hair deliberately or accidentally. Therefore, it is critical to keep chemical relaxer off your scalp. I have a technique I want to share it with you. I use it for both relaxers and retouches; it allows as little of the chemical as possible to get on your scalp.

Very little chemical will get on your scalp using this smoothing technique. The hair is lifted up in sections and the comb goes through the hair. **DO NOT** roll the back of the comb against the scalp. The same caution must be taken with the "finger and palm" method. The hair is lifted up in sections, the chemical is painted on with a brush and the comb presses the chemical against a gloved hand.

Now, I say all that to say this, I still believe the salon is best the place for performing chemical relaxer services for 5 very indisputable reasons.

Reason 1

The hairdresser can see your entire head when applying the chemical relaxer.

Reason 2

The salon provides a complete and better rinse out as it is very important to remove all traces of the chemical after the treatment.

Reason 3

Rinsing in the shower invites contact of the chemical to your entire body; salon sinks keep chemicals away from the body.

Reason 4

Laying your head over the sink backwards ensures minimal relaxer contact with your face.

Reason 5

It is far less stressful; it is more convenient; it is easier.

Remember, the most common form of hair loss is preventable meaning it did not have to happen and you initiated it. If you understand how to apply relaxers you should be able to prevent any hair loss caused by improper chemical application.

Cathy's Recommended Technique for Applying and Smoothing Chemical Relaxers

1. First put on gloves to protect your hands!

2. Then, divide your hair into about four to five sections. Clip each section out of the way.

3. Next, remove the clip off the section of hair you will be working with and divide it into smaller sections, about ¼" to ½" of hair to apply the chemical. Use the clip to keep all but the targeted section of hair out of the way.

4. Follow manufacturer instructions for properly preparing the chemical relaxer treatment.

5. Hold the targeted section of hair in the hand, and use the color applicator brush to apply the chemical first to one side of the hair section, about ¼" to ½" from the scalp. Carefully avoiding contact with the skin. Apply the chemical only to the new growth if this is a retouch or apply on the entire hair shaft if the chemical is intended to straighten the complete hair shaft.

6. Next, lift the hair section up and apply the relaxer to the underside of the hair section, again, keeping it about ¼" to ½" from the scalp.

7. To smooth the chemical, use the fingers and thumb to press the chemical through the hair. Use an upward motion to bring the chemical through the new growth. This technique is similar to picking up small objects off a table. Place the hair between the thumb and fingers and squeeze together then move upward on the section of hair. The comb can be used also in an upward motion against the palm of the gloved hand so it stays off the scalp.

8. After the allotted time for processing the hair is reached, the chemical is rinsed from the hair to remove all traces of the product and the hair is neutralized.

Summary

The textbook used for instruction on applying chemical relaxer is *approved by the licensing board for cosmetologists.*

The licensing board approved procedure *invites excessive* relaxer *chemical contact with the scalp.*

The proper technique for smoothing chemicals *will allow minimum skin contact.*

It is your responsibility to avoid skin damage caused by relaxer contact. *You are the one who will live with resulting hair loss so avoid it at all cost.*

4. Transition to Natural Hair
steps and tips for great natural hair

Just like a natural woman

The controversy over straightening afro-textured hair is woven throughout our history. A'Lelia Bundles' book entitled, *On Her Own Ground—The Life and Times of Madam C.J. Walker,* references an 1859 New York Times article about an assembly held in a rented hall to demonstrate a new *hair straightening process* where "the assembly turns to mayhem when a woman in the audience protests she would not desert her race to have straight hair."

The choice to straighten my hair at any time has never been motivated by a desire to have hair like white women or any other race with straight hair. I did it because it made caring for my hair a lot easier. When I made the decision to go natural, cutting my hair off was not an option. I had spent year after year carefully caring for and growing my long hair and to chop it off seemed ridiculous! So I had to figure out a way to keep the hair I gained while giving up chemical relaxers.

I had my last relaxer retouch on May 4, 2004. It was a scary feeling! But I had grown exhausted from the neverending effort it took to remind hairdressers about keeping the relaxer off my scalp. In addition, I had made the decision to never again give myself a retouch. My whole world changed when I decided to go natural. Trust me. I had no clue how I was going to go about making the transition after 35 years of chemical use. My hair would now have dual textures, and that meant each texture would have different needs. How would I handle these new issues?

I had dealt with my hair for as long as five months at a time without chemicals, but now I was determined to go beyond 20 weeks and have natural hair forever! I had to develop methods for converting my hair from chemically relaxed to natural hair. Sure, it had been done in the past by who knows how many Black women, but a proven method had never been documented.

So I found myself without a model and decided to create one so others would not have to reinvent the wheel. Every documented case of chemical relaxer abandonment seemed to require cutting off the chemically processed hair and or locing the natural hair; neither choice appealed to me. I love long straight hair and I was determined to keep all of my hair while making the transition.

Why natural is better for you

The reasons for giving up chemical relaxers to have natural hair are many and range from health to style to convenience. So before you set out to be completely au naturel you must address the transition issues. How will you care for your transforming hair? How will you style it? You will find the transition stages to be difficult as you face the challenges of hair styles that just do not work because of weather, length and varying textures. However, you take a positive approach to adapting to your transitioning hair and use these challenges to offset future hair issues. Most important, you have to stay focused on your hair transition goals.

Going natural without cutting off your relaxed hair is not easy because your afro-textured hair and relaxed hair have to coexist until your hair is completely transitioned. You will be tempted but please do not engage in that old method of grabbing the pressing comb and pressing your new growth just to make your transitioning hair easier to manage. This is the worst mistake you can make! It is important to use practical hair methods to protect the hair from excessive dryness and breakage. When I first set out on this mission, I gave myself three "do not break" rules: **Do not use a pressing comb; use only products that improve both the processed and natural hair; and use** *controlled handling* **to minimize hair shrinkage.**

Your transitioning hair cannot handle extreme heat

I am shocked to see articles advising us to use a pressing comb on our new growth. Obviously, the authors are not informed and do not understand the adverse effects their advice can have. The pressing comb, when it touches the chemically processed hair, will fry it. I have heard many stories about hairdressers and the pressing techniques used on Black women who have given up chemical relaxers— ignoring the fact that direct contact from a hot metal pressing comb destroys chemically processed hair. After this happens, the hair

Pressing comb use is forbidden when transitioning from chemically processed hair.

starts breaking at an abnormal rate. When you go back to the hairdresser and complain about your hair breakage, you are likely to get blamed for your hair's condition. Yet, it is their lack of knowledge about relaxed hair that has contributed to your hair problems. They just want to believe you have done something wrong and will not bother to investigate the problem from their vantage point. When in fact, it was indeed the use of a pressing comb on relaxed hair that caused your hair to break off. Chemically processed hair cannot tolerate the extreme heat generated by a pressing comb. Avoid this hair-damaging process and save your hair from excessive breakage. This includes irons heated by direct contact with a heat source such as fire or stove and plug-in pressing combs, either will contribute to the ever-increasing nightmare of your hair loss. This particular recommendation is tantamount to your hair's survival through the transitioning process.

Products that improve your hair must be used

Writing my *Ultra Black Hair Growth* book helped me realize the importance of clean hair. I knew the basics of clean hair, what shampoo to use, how often to shampoo, as well as proper conditioning techniques and minimizing appliance use. However, basic hair care techniques are no substitute for using good products. The products you use while transitioning your hair must work well for both of your hair types and be able to improve both natural and relaxed hair. Understand that products costing a small fortune are not indicative of a good product. Fancy ads and brand names also are not a guarantee of quality, hair-improving ingredients. If products that improve the hair are overlooked, excessive breakage will result. Although weak hair can break any where along the hair shaft, hair is more susceptible to breakage where the new growth meets the processed hair. Using products that improve the hair must strengthen the entire hair shaft especially hair where the natural part of the strand connects with the chemically processed part.

Products Required to Transition

Shampoo—should be formulated for dry damaged hair, chemically treated and or color-treated hair. Although your hair may be classified as none of the above, make sure the product you use on afro-textured hair is specified as such. If you find itchy scalp constantly plagues you, select a shampoo from the health food store that does not contain sodium lauryl sulfate (also known as sodium laurel sulfate) or its relative sodium laureth sulfate; both are known irritants to the skin and found in most commercial shampoo products.

Deep conditioner—improves the hair. A good deep conditioner is required weekly and must contain protein and oils. The external application of protein is necessary to make the hair stronger. The oils in a good deep conditioner will keep dry hair internally lubricated. There is no substitute for weekly deep conditioning.

Instant conditioner—smoothes your hair's cuticle. An instant conditioner can be left on the processed hair and the natural hair. I have found in order to smooth natural hair, especially at the roots during transition, something has to dry on the hair. The instant conditioner is not to be confused with your weekly deep conditioner because they perform two separate functions. Your instant conditioner will not improve the health of your hair. It will improve the texture so you can easily comb out with minimal breakage. The instant conditioner may contain Cetearyl alcohol, which is not drying to the skin and hair; or it may contain Cetyl alcohol, which closely resembles a component of the body's natural oil Sebum. Both are used as an emulsifier and emollient. Other ingredients in your instant conditioner may increase hair breaking. However, these two ingredients do not negatively affect a healthy hair condition.

Moisturizer—locks in moisture. Moisturizer is critical to minimizing dry hair breakage. It must penetrate the hair shaft to get to the source of dryness. It must also contain oils that lubricate the hair but do not make the hair greasy. If the product you choose contains mineral oil or petroleum switch to one that does not. Moisture must get to the cortex, the source of dry hair. Mineral oil and petroleum only lay on the surface of the hair and prevent moisture from penetrating.

Use of controlled handling

The most difficulty you may encounter as you transition will likely occur after a hair washing. Using the *controlled handling* method will minimize tangling after the natural hair gets 6 to 8 inches and beyond. *Controlled handling* is the procedure I use for preparing the hair for shampooing, comb out, flat-ironing, blow drying or other styling methods. This simple technique keeps the hair in a relatively straight position at the roots. Afro-textured hair shrinks when it gets wet, and if it dries uncombed, it will mat up. Your goal is to prevent the hair from drying out before you are ready to work with it. Before you wash your hair it is already stretched out. To reduce over stressing the hair, take advantage of the already straight hair and keep it as straight as possible while it is wet.

If there is failure to handle hair in a controlled fashion, wet hair starts to dry quickly. As you manipulate hair on one side of the head, the other side will dry out requiring rewetting and therefore more pulling on the hair to remove tangles. When afro-textured hair shrinks the coil condenses, and this is where most of the tangling occurs. This can be prevented by keeping the hair together.

The best controlled handling tool

The hair scrunchy is a hair separating tool. They hold the hair very well. The best ones are cloth with an elastic band inside that stretches over the hair like rubber bands to keep the hair in place without damaging the hair strands. Putting cloth scrunchies on the hair before it becomes wet allows hair to stay less coiled at the roots. The elastic-filled scrunchy allows the hair to stay together and keeps it stretched out. The hair that is bound by scrunchy bands is unable to dry fast allowing you to work with other hair without rushing to get to all the hair before it dries and coils. Each of the scrunchies used during shampoo and conditioning, can be removed individually to apply instant conditioner and to comb through, followed by braiding or twisting and clamping each hair section to prepare for styling.

The controlled handling procedure

Before you shampoo your hair, part it into four or five sections and put scrunchie bands on them. I have found the fewer the scrunchies the better because you may want to remove the bands one at a time for thorough rinsing; you will need to replace them. I loop mine over the hair sections about three times so they are loose enough to move just slightly down the hair section when the hair is manipulated. Exercise great care when removing the scrunchy. Grabbing the entire scrunchy and rolling down the hair may catch coily hair and result in breakage. Avoid scrunchies connected with metal. When you put them on they tend to break the hair. Wash and condition the hair using the *controlled handling* procedure. The only time you do not use it is when you are coloring your hair. Dye needs to be completely rinsed from the hair. So binding it while dying may make it difficult to thoroughly rinse, and hair may come out tye-dyed.

Here is my recommended transition hair care procedure:

Cathy's Natural Hair Care Procedure

- **Weekly shampoo**—using one shampoo not two or three as this leads to excessive dryness where the oils are stripped from the hair by too much suds. Select shampoo designed for dry damaged hair, color-treated hair or chemically treated hair. Use *controlled handling* to minimize tangling.

- **Deep condition**—weekly with a product that contains protein and oils that improve the hair.

- **Protein treatments**—periodically or when you notice more breakage than normal.

- **Prepare the hair**—(covered in the next chapter) before styling, apply an instant conditioner to the hair and carefully comb the new growth as well as all natural hair while wet to detangle and to prevent matting. Comb just enough to separate the hairs so they unwind.

- **Maintain throughout the week**—by lightly misting the hair ends with your dew moisturizer and applying just a small dot of creme moisturizer daily to the hair ends to prevent the hair from reverting.

- **Style as you desire**

- **Repeat weekly**

The basics of Black hair care are discussed in my book *Ultra Black Hair Growth II*. I recommend you read it to gain a good understanding of Black hair basics before you begin to transition to your natural hair. The routines of caring for natural hair or proper hair care during transition stages change only slightly. The biggest challenge with natural hair will be how you get and keep the hair straight.

Summary

Do not use pressing combs on chemically processed hair.

Straightening new growth with a pressing comb is forbidden.

To improve natural hair and chemically processed hair, you must strengthen it.

Good hair care techniques are not a substitute for good hair care products.

Pricey products are not indicative of quality products.

Use *controlled handling* to keep natural hair from retracting when wet.

5. Value-Added Transition Tips
long-term maintenance for your hair

Extra care will make a huge difference in your hair

Do I have "bad hair days" since I do not relax any more? That depends on what you call "bad hair days." My hair is not as smooth all the time as I would like so I just work with what I have. And since I do not work for corporate America I can wear my hair in nontraditional ways. If I were not afraid of losing my hair, I would probably relax my hair indefinitely. But the risk is too frightening and I will not take that chance. I gave up the practice not because I wanted to, but because I had to. There is no longer the temptation to relax my hair even though my current hair treatments require a greater investment of effort and time.

To chemically relax your hair or to keep it natural is a decision you personally have to make. The only way to prevent immediate thinning hair caused by chemicals is to give up relaxers, perms and any and all chemicals you put on your scalp! My hair is still thick, full and beautiful after all these years because I made an informed decision about my hair's future. It is not an easy task but I consider it well worth it. Like anything in life, the amount of reward is weighted against the amount of investment.

Will aging cause my beautiful hair to thin? Does past chemical use affect the hair in the long run? Without long term research I do not know what the future holds. I made the decision to give up chemical treatments so I would keep my hair. Now, I can teach every Black woman who follows the methods in this book how they too can keep their hair! Weigh what is important to you. Hopefully the insight you gain from this book will not only open your eyes but encourage you throughout the challenge. So you can have great success with your hair.

Expect longer wash times

The biggest chore in transitioning to your natural hair will be wash day. Washing your hair in the shower is still the best place unless you can install a hairdresser sink in one of your bathrooms. I was fortunate to have a second bathroom where I did install this very handy sink. It allows all of my hair washing and rinsing to be performed in an inclined position, which keeps liquid hair products from running in my face.

Getting shampoo through natural hair to the scalp to get rid of bacteria, oil and sweat is harder when your shampoo is a thick consistency. Dilute it so it will get through to the scalp properly.

Here are some other tips and steps.

1. Purchase a color applicator bottle with a nozzle on it. Pour shampoo in the bottle until ¼ full.

2. Add enough water to make it runny, then shake to mix.

3. Point the nozzle directly at the scalp in each scrunchy band and squeeze out the contents.

4. Manipulate each area under the scrunchy with your finger tips to produce suds.

5. Rinse each section carefully. Temporarily remove each

scrunchy from the hair one at a time to ensure no shampoo or debris remains on the hair; then replace them.

6. Use *controlled handling* each time you shampoo.

Applying the deep conditioner on the hair will be easy with *controlled handling* since you are basically just putting the most conditioner on the hair ends and hair sections that are hanging on the outside of the scrunchy. Apply a small amount of conditioner to the hair next to the scalp but it is not necessary to put a lot on as all the hair will be put under your processing cap to deep condition. The hair with conditioner on it will spread conditioner to the hair close to the scalp as well. Be sure to use your hooded dryer when you deep condition to swell the hair open so the conditioner penetrates the hair to get to the source of the dryness.

How much breakage is too much?

Chemically treated hair stretches out when it is wet and is prone to breaking off easily when pulled or overstressed by combs and brushes. Therefore, do very little combing on chemically processed wet hair. On the other hand, comb out is required very soon after you shampoo and condition natural hair to stretch it out. This pulling and stretching will inevitably cause stress breakage. People often ask me how much breakage is too much breakage? They ask about the 100 hairs a day principle. The truth is I do not count hair on the sink or in the comb and neither should you. Instead you should look at how much of each type of hair is on the sink after combing dry hair. Is it lots of little ends? Is it chunks of hair? Is it lots of long strands and broken pieces?

Expect stress breakage. Simply combing hair produces stress breakage because you are pulling on the hair. Expect it. Straightening natural hair produces stress breakage. So there is no confusion in knowing which type of breakage is cause for concern, I have defined two types.

Stress Breakage—Forget the comb theory you see in magazine ads that suggest strands of hair in your comb is a problem. If you have natural hair or chemically processed hair, you will stress your hair when you comb it out. The goal is to minimize hair loss when it is stressed. Finding a few long hairs on the sink and in the comb, depending on how long it has been since your last chemical retouch and the health of your hair, can be from two different causes. Hair breaking may be due to stressing the hair or a result of dryness, damage or weakness. Combing both natural hair and relaxed hair will produce stress breakage. Stress breakage should be the least of your concerns. It is severe breakage resulting from a failure to minimize the inevitable that makes the hair shorter.

Severe Breakage—To better identify severe breakage, stand backwards over your bathroom sink and comb non-wet hair by running the comb through the hair several times so any hair that falls will fall onto the sink. Look for broken hair pieces all over the sink and your clothes. The little short hairs are hair ends that are breaking off in most cases due to extremely dry hair in need of more moisture. The longer pieces may result from an improper chemical application or poor hair maintenance. So hair all over the sink is what you do not want to see.

Severe breakage happens when the hair is damaged and weak. Lots of broken pieces of hair that are long and short and lots of variations in between signal severe hair breakage and is cause for concern. This breakage is often caused by improper care or from an improper chemical treatment. It is not difficult to see why hair damage results when you understand what a chemical hair straightener applied to hair does. The FDA, when classifying depilatories and hair straighteners states:

> "These ingredients cause degradation of hair keratin and deterioration of hair fibers to a jelly-like mass that can easily be removed by wiping or scraping."

Severe breakage from a chemical may in some cases be remedied by applying a protein treatment, but it is not a sure cure if the hair is damaged beyond strengthening.

Expect little knots

Natural afro-textured hair is coily and it can coil together any where along the hair shaft. Ten to 20 hairs or more will wind together almost like it is trying to loc. Those little knots we find in our hair from time to time in the middle of the hair shaft will become more prominent as you transition to natural hair. Nekhena Evans defines them in her book *Hairlocking: Everything You Need to Know* as 'rebellious hair' indicating the 'budding phase.' This is a natural process for afro-textured hair. *Controlled handling* and leaving an instant conditioner on the hair to smooth the hair cuticle will minimize the number of little hair knots.

Extending your retouch

To make hair look nice continually, you must rise to the challenge of caring for both the roots and the old relaxed hair, keeping in mind their different hair care needs. In the past, I extended my retouches for 4 to 5 months successfully, but I knew that I could extend retouches longer. To give up chemical relaxers required I master extending a retouch, even though I never planned to do one on my hair ever again.

Extending a retouch means caring for your hair in such a way that it will remain in optimum condition. This can become a challenge with the natural hair at the roots and chemically processed hair on the ends. The purpose of extending the retouch keeps chemicals off your head for as long as possible or forever. You can extend it for 12 weeks and beyond if proper techniques are used along with quality products that improve the hair. So do not purchase additional product marketed as *extending the retouch* because good maintenance products will give good results.

Extending a retouch means straightening the roots or new growth so they match the relaxed hair. The longer the hair gets, the more tangled it becomes especially where the two textures meet. Your goal will be to make the two textures similar in look and feel.

Basics for Extending a Retouch

1. After washing the hair, soften the new growth by moisturizing it with a good crème moisturizer. Start by parting the hair in small sections. Put a small amount of crème moisturizer on your fingertips and rub them together. Apply the crème from your fingertips to the new growth by pressing it through the hair. (Sort of like picking up something with your fingers.) Instead of focusing on the hair, traditional hair care methodology encouraged putting products on the scalp. Do not oil your scalp or use your crème moisturizer on your scalp. The moisturize goes on the hair only. (Note: If you intend to use a flat iron or blowdryer to straighten, you can also use an instant conditioner on the new growth to soften and smooth.)

2. Comb through each section of the new growth after application. Be sure the new growth hair is combed out wet to remove tangles and allow gentle stretching.

3. Carefully handle processed hair to prevent unnecessary stress and breaking.

4. Avoid grease, mineral oil or petroleum based products as they coat the hair and lock out moisture. And you will know when moisture is being locked out because the oil or grease will lay on the surface of the hair and come off on your hand when you touch your hair.

5. Temporarily straighten the new growth so it matches the chemical hair texture.

6. **NEVER** use a pressing comb or stove-heated irons because they destroy the hair cuticle of chemically processed hair!

7. Use products that penetrate the hair.

8. Use products that smooth the texture.

Preparing the hair before styling

Now that you have washed your hair, what do you do? When you straighten natural hair you will want it to be stretched out, so the hair dries in a less coiled or more straight way. After a washing, the tight texture of my hair forces me to do more than simply comb my hair out before straightening it. So I had to come up with a way to prepare my hair for straightening. This is the method I use:

1. Apply an instant conditioner to smooth the texture of the hair.
2. Comb out all tangles.
3. Position the hair for straight styling.

Positioning the hair can take two forms.

1. You can braid or plait the hair.
2. You can twist the hair and clasp it.

When you prepare the hair for styling, less breakage will occur. These steps will help keep breakage to a minimum.

1. After the hair has been shampooed and deep conditioned, use an instant conditioner to smooth the texture before combing. Oils from your deep conditioner can weigh the hair down but are required to lubricate the inside of the hair. Occasionally, you may choose to reshampoo the hair to remove excess oil for a more bouncy styling, but it is not recommended that you reshampoo after each deep conditioner.

2. After applying the instant conditioner, start the comb out at the ends to detangle the hair; then gradually work up the hair section until you get to the hair closest to the scalp. Then comb down the entire hair strand to ensure tangles are eliminated. Combing the instant conditioner through the hair is not to evenly distribute conditioner. This step

facilitates comb out by smoothing the hair cuticle to minimize breakage.

A wide tooth comb is still recommended for afro-textured or coily hair; however, it may miss many tangles in natural hair. Carefully use a small-toothed comb to remove tangles.

If you still have a lot of chemical relaxer on your hair, comb through the new growth and avoid combing the processed hair because processed hair is often weak from chemical processing and is prone to breaking when it is pulled.

3. Perform one of the following: Braid or plait the hair loosely so it dries quickly or twist and clasp small sections of hair in preparation for salon straightening. If you do roller sets, you can take each of these sections of the hair and add your rollers.

Braids when dried and taken down can produce beautiful hair waves. If you like a natural wavy look, braids may be the way to go for this part of the procedure.

Home hair straightening—If you dry natural hair in a stretched position the coils shrink less as it dries. For home hair straightening, I recommend braiding or plaiting the hair before straightening. Only use this technique when you are doing your hair at home; removing the braids may be too time consuming for your stylist. Also, I prefer to wash and straighten my hair all in the same day as opposed to waiting overnight for the hair to dry, which can create more work because of additional pulling and stretching.

Blowdryer straightening—At home, if done correctly, will remove tangles and leave the hair relatively smooth. The blowdryer will need to be operated on the higher settings to straighten afro-textured hair and can be used with a comb attachment to stretch and separate the hair as it dries. Use of a brush during blowdrying is acceptable because it holds the hair in a straight position and minimizes blowdryer time. Just make sure the hair texture is smooth enough to allow the brush to glide easily through the hair. After you braid your hair, minimize drying time with the blowdryer by using a hooded dryer to dry the hair more quickly so it can be blowdried more quickly. Blowdrying offers the best straightening results.

Flat iron straightening—Works best when you still have only about 2 to 3 inches of new growth. If you decide to flat iron and not blowdry, expect more tangles and more little knots in the hair all along the hair shaft.

Salon hair straightening—Natural hair must be stretched out as much as possible, especially when you go to the salon. Most salons will shampoo your hair the traditional way; so expect the hair to be loose all over and prone to tangling if it is not prepared before straightening. If you go to a salon and the washing does not include preparing the hair for blowdrying, expect your hair to break more. So talk with your hairdresser and request the *controlled handling* technique before your hair service begins. And if you are blessed to have a hairdresser who does not mind if you wash your own hair, you can twist your hair and clasp it into small sections and prepare it yourself for straightening. This ensures your hair stays out of the way for easier handling by the stylist. Remember to cover your hair with a plastic processing cap to keep your hair from drying out before your appointment.

Many stylists will use a brush to straighten the hair while it is being blown dry. This is the only time I allow a brush in my hair. Blowdrying with a brush to stretch out the hair while drying requires skill as the hairdresser has to make the coily hair resemble the relaxed hair. Now that my hair is virtually chemical free and healthy, very little breakage occurs when blown dry with a brush.

Hair color and natural hair

When you have natural hair your main concern is to keep hair color off your scalp. Hair color is also a chemical that can cause hair thinning.

In the past, when I relaxed my hair I would immediately color my hair with a product that did not contain ammonia or peroxide. It would go right to the open hair shaft and not just lay on the hair's surface. Now that I no longer relax my hair I apply neutralizing shampoo. It helps reduce hair color residue that may be left on the surface of the hair from transferring to my towels.

Use caution with heated hair appliances

Your natural hair becomes stronger each week without chemicals becoming more healthy and resilient. So you want to make sure it stays that way and use care when using heated hair appliances. Blow drying and flat ironing are effective at straightening new growth; however, during the initial transition stages you will want to eliminate sources of dry hair and avoid techniques that may promote dryness; so use the blow dryer only when absolutely necessary. Initially, when you have a lot of the chemical remaining on the hair, another option is to sit under the hooded dryer, gently separate the hair with your fingers or a comb, and smooth each section of hair with your hands. Combing ever so gently when you encounter tangles and matting at the roots. Early on, if you decide to use the blow dryer to straighten the roots then flat iron on the rest of your hair, you may see a lot of breakage. If you use the flat iron do not use the blow dryer.

Controlling the elements

Rain and moisture will totally revert natural hair that has been straightened. As much as you may oppose the idea, carry one of those silly rain caps in your purse at all times. It will save your hair and all your hard work. Also, keep an umbrella around: one at home, one at your office and one in your car. You never know when it will rain. If rain partially reverts your straight hair, keep in mind that you are having your hair straightened weekly and if the unexpected dampness ruins your hair you have only 1 to 2 days before you get your hair straightened again.

Humidity is your worst enemy so your beautiful scarves come in handy here. The sole purpose is to keep the humidity from directly affecting your hair as much as possible. If you are going to be outside for long periods of time in a humid environment there is little recourse. Otherwise, if you are going in and out of a humid environment or if you live in areas that are close to large bodies of water, your scarf will provide the best protection when you go outside. If you have a job working outside choose a style that can be pulled back and held in place to keep your hair from getting poofy. After you spend hours getting your natural hair straight styled, you want it to last for more than one day.

Here are some suggestions for helping keep your natural hair straight for several days.

When you shower—Use two processing caps together on your head or an extra heavy shower cap. Pull it over your ears to prevent water from getting on the edges. Your night head wrap can also be left on the hair before adding the shower cap as added protection to prevent those one or two hair strands from slipping out from under the cap and getting wet. Leave the bathroom before you remove the shower cap to prevent steam in the room from ruining your straight hair style.

When you sleep—To keep straightened hair straight, you can achieve full and fluffy hair the next day if you tie your hair in an upward direction with a scarf (it does not have to be silk). You will need to get the hair on the top of your head by bending forward or even lying back against the arm rest on the couch where you are slightly inclined. Take a full size scarf and fold it into a triangle. Wrap the scarf around your head from the back to the front, tying it firmly in the front so the hair is pushed up and not flattened down when you sleep. Use a minimum of four large hair pins to help keep the scarf from sliding off during the night when you sleep. The hair hanging out the top of the scarf can further be covered with a sleeping cap or bonnet.

If you prefer a flatter look, purchase a wave cap that fits snugly over your head; then put the sleeping cap on over that. Start by using your hands to part the hair in the back of your head down the middle. Lay one side over the other side and secure with hair pins or flat hair clips, then cover with the wave cap. The only disadvantage of wrapping one side of hair over another side of hair is you usually get a fold in the middle of your hair.

Swimming—Black women want to enjoy a dip in the pool too, but the concern over chlorine drying and breaking chemically processed hair and water reverting natural hair is a major concern. Using a "pool cap" does not prevent water from getting to your hair and was never intended for that purpose. The real purpose was to keep hair out of the pool, but no one seems to even wear the "rubber cap" these days. To minimize the threat of drying out chemically processed hair you would be wise to shampoo your hair immediately after getting out of the pool and then apply a good moisturizer. Depending on how often you swim it is recommended you use a clarifying shampoo periodically to remove the residue left behind by chlorine treated waters and always deep condition weekly to ensure the health of your hair.

For the natural hair woman who refuses to sit poolside, not only should you incorporate the information above but before you take the plunge your style must include *controlled handling*. Braiding or plaiting natural hair is the most viable option. *Controlled handling* is required to position natural hair before it gets wet to prevent coily hair retracting which in turn minimizes excessive pulling, tangling, matting and breaking.

Exercise—Sweating out your edges will always be of concern to the girl who straightens her natural hair. I love going to the gym for my daily workout, and I refuse to give it up just because I now have natural hair. Yes, my scalp sweats and the hair close to the scalp slightly reverts. This does not bother me because I know I will have it redone in the next few days since I wash and straighten weekly. But before I go to the gym, I always pull my hair to the back of my head, then twist it and clip it up on top of my head. I also pin up any hair hanging down around my face on top of my head to minimize exposure to perspiration which can cause the hair strand and roots to revert.

Schedule your workout routines around your hair care treatments. Save heavy exercise for the days prior to hair treatments and avoid working out immediately after your hair has been straightened and styled. You do not want to use flat iron or a curling iron daily to smooth the edges reverted by perspiration just try to conceal the edges until your next hair appointment.

Wearing your hair up may help you make it through those last few days before your next appointment. To help smooth the edges try using a dot of lotion crème on them with what is left on the hands after applying it to the ends. Just an FYI: perspiration is a natural body fluid and does not on its own dry the hair out or cause hair breakage!

> ∽
> **Perspiration is a natural body fluid and does not on its own dry the hair out or cause hair breakage.**
> ∽

Styling options

I am always asked to give suggestions on styling hair, but I can only tell you how I style my hair. With so many different lengths, shapes and textures, it is impossible for me to provide options for every individual hair type. I prefer wearing my hair straight, in a ponytail, in an up-do, in a French braid and occasionally in twists. During the growing out phrase of my transition to natural hair, the ponytail was my preferred style because it kept my hair from appearing poofy. Ponytails are a good styling option when growing out the chemical because they require very little manipulation and handling resulting in less stress on the hair.

Twists are an excellent style when growing out the chemical because you can visually blend the two textures together. Having someone else do them for me makes them look better than the ones I did so I did not wear them often. However, I did love the style. Also one of the best books for styling natural hair is *Plaited Glory: For Colored Girls Who've Considered Braids, Locs and Twists* by Lonnice Brittenum Bonner. Her book provides excellent techniques for how to twist style natural hair. She also provides instruction for locing natural hair, if you decide to go that route.

If you choose to blend fake hair into your natural hair for braid styles, you are going to experience breakage. Fake hair braided in with your own hair does not allow your hair to get the treatments it needs because fake hair functions as a buffer. Maintenance products must reach the hair to improve it and if you use fake hair when you braid, the fake hair absorbs the products and robs your hair of the maximum benefit of treatments.

Whether you choose to have your hair relaxed or natural, the tips in this chapter will help you attain and maintain the healthiest hair possible.

Summary

Stress breakage is inevitable when the hair is pulled by combs and brushes.

Severe breakage is what we need to be concerned about.

Extending your retouch is critical when you decide to transition from chemicals

6. Sister Talk
comments and concerns, questions and answers

Sister Talk features casual conversation about the issues and concerns many Black women face with their hair. It includes comments and questions I have received from my customers. In the Question and Answer (Q&A) Section, I answer some of my customer's toughest questions and help them find solutions to their hair problems. As you will see, we all face similar problems with our hair—you are not alone.

I would love to hear from you. Share your hair triumphs or issues with me at www.ultrablackhair.com. Together, we can save our beautiful black hair.

戉

Katie (not her real name) called and told the story of how her sister had applied a relaxer contrary to her mother's beliefs and it ruined her hair. She said her mom created this "borax soap" mixture and proceeded to scrub her sister's hair. Katie and her mother believed that this rough scrubbing and the soapy mixture had truly removed the chemical from her sister's hair because her mother said it was no longer on the hair. It had to be the rough texture of her sister's hair that made her believe that the relaxer was completely removed from the hair, but what had really happened was the cuticle was so ruffed up by the harsh soap that it looked unprocessed.

There is no product on the market that can remove a

> ❧
> **There is no product on the market that can remove a chemical relaxer from the hair once it has been applied.**
> ❧

chemical from the hair once it has been applied. Hair straighteners or perm chemicals permanently change the hair structure internally and externally.

Scrubbing the hair only destroyed the top layer of hair, the cuticle, making it appear that the relaxer was "removed." The cuticle appearing "nappy" presents a false sense of security. Don't make the mistake of thinking that once your hair is chemically processed that you can "scrub it out." The only way to remove a relaxer from chemically processed hair is to do one of two things: cut if off or let it grow out!

We have so many questions about relaxing our hair and very few answers. This first section of Sister Talk presents some very shocking but familiar scenarios we face as Black women when we choose to chemically relax.

☙

SISTER TALK - "MY DAUGHTER'S MISSING SIDES"

"I let my eleven year old daughter talk me into allowing her to go to a friend's beautician for her relaxer retouch so she could do a twist/up-do pony tail the first week of school. Now just two months later her hair has fallen out around her edges and is no longer the full, thick hair she used to have. I have always done her relaxer retouch and it has never fallen out or even broken off. I started relaxing her hair when she was going on ten years old so she had worn a relaxer for over a year without problems. What could have happened this time and how do I fix it?"

☙

SISTER TALK - "I'VE HAD BALD SIDES FOR YEARS"

"My hair has been balding for several years now. It will grow back a little then it starts falling off again. I have been to doctors who can't really tell me what is going on. One doctor told me that my body thinks my hair is a virus and it is shedding to get rid of the virus. I was taking shots for that but I stopped after about 2 years. The next doctor I went to said I was grieving from the loss of my parents in other words it was my nerves. He gave me some kind of prescription that looks like petroleum to use on my scalp. Now, I just don't know what is going on. I know it will grow but I don't know how to care for it so it will grow. All I know is that my scalp is either itching or burning most of the time. I am at my wits end. And yes, I did use chemicals years ago before this happened. My sides were balding when I started using relaxers but not as bad as now. My hair became thin on top after I started using relaxers but now I am bald and it starts from the crown of my head and goes straight down the middle until the back of my head. I have some growth in the back but from the very bottom of my scalp I have noticed the hair balding from the bottom up where my hair was always very full in the back but was thin on top. If I still have some hair in the thin places and I stop relaxing my hair do you think I can salvage the rest of the hair to at least make it look decent?"

CR

SISTER TALK - "WOMEN AT MY SALON ARE ALL COMPLAINING ABOUT THINNING HAIR"

"I have been using your products since August 2004. My hair was beautiful (healthy, shoulder length) until I decided to dye it. I did not use the product that you highly recommended. I really regret this. I am sorry to say that I had serious hair breakage. I have not dyed my hair since December 2004, and I want to cry when I see the hair damage that has been caused by the hair dye. I got bored with my dark hair color so a very popular hairdresser recommended "Textures and Tones™." I used the light brown and I even had a professional dye my hair. You are right when you claim that not every professional knows what they are doing. I demanded my hairdresser to quit using Marcel curling irons on my hair and I referred her to your website. After reading another hair book I began to experiment with hair products and this turned out to be a huge mistake. I now realize that hair dye changes the texture of your hair making it drier than ever---and certain styling methods can make the hair drier. I do not want to cut my hair, but I am not the type of person who wants to simply cover up mistakes (i.e. breakage from the hair dye). I'm not patient, either. I learned the hard way to only stay within your recommendation for hair growth. I really want long hair. Meanwhile, I noticed that in addition to my hair, other women who come to the same beauty shop were complaining about their hair thinning around the nape, sides and temples. Otherwise, there is hair growth in the other areas. I cannot pinpoint what this could be, but our hairdresser is aware of this hair loss. What do you think could be causing this?"

44

&#x06;

SISTER TALK - "IS THE HAIR ROOT DEAD OR JUST STUNTED?"

"I'm just trying to figure out if my hair's roots are stunted or dead. It hasn't grown in a while but my head is not completely bald. Do you go bald when the root is dead or does your hair just not grow anymore and whatever hair is already there is all that will ever be there in the future? What can you tell me?"

&#x06;

SISTER TALK - "MY HAIRLINE IS VERY THIN"

"My hair history is very bad. I have relaxed hair (self relaxers done for years, not always the same brand and sometimes left in for too long). I dyed my hair myself once about two and a half years ago. I wore braids in my hair for about a year straight, then I started to wear glued in tracks. I used to always brush my hair when it was wet. I tried to keep up with trims and I abused my hair with heat in unimaginable ways. I just did almost everything your book advices against. I also have been wasting money on different shampoos and conditioners. The problems with my hair are first of all my hairline is very thin and I'm going to a dermatologist next week to see if my roots are dead from braiding for too long. My hair only grows in the back and it doesn't grow much. The ends of my hair are frizzy and I have a lot of fly-away. I'm just trying to get my hair healthy again. The growth will come with good health and "common sense" and with how I take care of it. What can you tell me to help me in that process of healthy hair with my hair history? I would also like to know what you would advise me to do if I'm trying to grow my relaxer out. It's about time for another one but I'm thinking of just growing it out, but I'm not so sure because of all the stories of hair loss when trying this. If you don't use heat what do you do? Please tell me everything you can to get me through my hair problems."

‍ॐ

SISTER TALK - "SUDDEN HAIR LOSS AND THE DOCTOR WANTS TO INJECT MY SCALP!"

"I washed my hair as normal and used a protein treatment since my hair was breaking more than usual. I followed directions exactly as I done before. When I rinsed it out I noticed a little tangling and applied some UBH Crème and let it air dry. The following morning I carefully comb out the tangles. I was feeling around my hair and scalp to make sure my hair was fully dried before I flat ironed it. I noticed a dime size bald spot almost to the middle of my head and even bigger patch on the very back of my head! Of course I was crying! I went to see a dermatologist and he said I have Alopecia Areata from an unknown cause and prescribed some type of ointment for my scalp once a day. It's been almost a month now and I am seeing some little hairs starting to come back. I am supposed to follow up with the doctor later this month and he may inject my scalp if needed. I'm so frustrated because I started to see some progress and something like this happens. I haven't had a relaxer since this happened and I'm too afraid to relax it. Now it's breaking a little more since I'm way overdue for one. Could stress cause the hair to break off all the way to the scalp? I'm doing some research on the internet and can't find anything about stress and hair. Have any advice for me?"

‍ॐ

SISTER TALK - "WEAK SPOT AT CROWN OF HEAD"

"I have a weak spot at the top of my head, about the size of a quarter, where the hair is shorter than the rest of my hair. I think this spot has gotten this way due to the use of micro braids. The spot is improving, however, it is still very noticeable. My hair is cut in a bob and I was thinking about pulling it back into a ball, using no heat and only conditioning and washing it to see if will speed up the growing process.

Do you have any suggestions regarding my condition?"

☙

SISTER TALK - "TEMPLES GONE, NOTHING THERE"

"The sides of my head around my temple area seem to be losing hair to the point of practically nothing being there. I'm not on any medications at all, nor am I stressed. I've even added more water and vitamins to my diet, so I can't figure out why my sides are doing this. I used a protein treatment a couple of weeks back. I really need a word of good advice! Please, if you could recommend anything (Aloe Vera, Tea Tree oil), ANYTHING AT ALL that could help before this problem gets worse, I would sincerely appreciate it."

☙

SISTER TALK - "MY 3-YEAR OLD IS BALD AFTER I USED A KIDDY PERM ON HER!"

"I have a three year old daughter and I made the terrible mistake of putting a kiddy perm on her hair because it was so unmanageable. Well, that ended up breaking her hair and she is going bald. I'm not sure what to do to save it now and I want to restore her hair. So can you please give me some suggestions?"

Because there are still so many questions about relaxing the hair, this next section of Sister Talk I answer questions about getting relaxing right! Here Sisters speak out again. These are their questions and my answers when queried about relaxers.

SISTER TALK
QUESTIONS & ANSWERS

SISTER TALK - "MY CHEMICAL PLANT JOB"

Q: I work at a chemical manufacturing company and we do not make relaxers, however I just found out that sodium hydroxide, a caustic substance is found in relaxers. Do you know that it is also a main ingredient in the harsh chemicals we sell to kill bacteria off machines and steel appliances? I refuse to expose myself to caustic chemicals. I never knew relaxers were so harsh. I am in complete shock. No wonder we do not have hair. I do not know what I am going to do but I refuse to put another caustic treatment in my hair. I have seen the white residue after it dries and it can eat your skin off as well as your hair.

A: Yes I do know about the chemical in relaxers. And I also know everything in our lives is made up of chemicals.

When you **wash your clothes** you use a chemical.

When you **shampoo your hair**, you use chemicals.

When you **shower or bathe with soap**, you use chemicals.

When you **drink city water**, it is treated with chemicals.

When you **brush your teeth with toothpaste** the container states "call poison control if you swallow more than what is used to brush your teeth" because it too is a chemical.

The **plastic wrap you put around your food** and put in the microwave contains chemicals.

It is no wonder we die of so many different forms of cancer with all the chemicals that are introduced to our bodies year after year. We use

48

these products without thinking anything of it. The truth of the matter is that some chemicals are necessary in our lives, for instance we use them to kill bacteria that can prevent the spread of disease, but used inappropriately can result in death.

The problem is that relaxers are misapplied. Relaxers NEVER should come in contact with the scalp. It is the ignorance of people who use them that causes the problem. Keep in mind that many things we use in our day to day lives contain chemicals, from your soap to your shampoo. If they are appropriately used damage can be averted.

☙

SISTER TALK - "CAN I GO 'NO LYE' RELAXER TO LYE?"

Q: I've been using regular 'no lye' relaxer for years and I wanted a mild strength because I need a relaxer every four weeks. Yesterday, I changed chemicals and bought 'lye' mild strength relaxer. I had it professionally done. If I do it again should I use the 'no lye' version? I really need your help. Please guide me.

A: It is NOT recommended that you change between "lye" and "no lye" as they are both two different chemicals! It is not in my best interest to tell you to use the "no lye" again because I really don't want to be responsible for you having problems with your hair by switching chemicals. My experience and philosophy is you can change from "lye" to "no lye" for hair that is in otherwise good condition, but it is not a good idea to change back OR to go back and forth. Had I been making the initial call, I would have told you NEVER to switch to the other product in the first place. Also a chemical relaxer every four weeks is too often to do relaxer retouches. You are destroying your hair!

CR

SISTER TALK - "I CHANGED MY RELAXER FROM 'NO LYE' TO 'LYE' NOW MY HAIR IS BREAKING!"

Q: I have just relaxed my hair. I changed from 'no lye' to a 'lye' based relaxer. I was really noticing that my hair had too much buildup, and it was growing dull. I noticed it had been getting worse over time while using the 'no lye' relaxer. Should I follow your rule to stick with what I am using now to avoid further damage? I just hope that this experience is just a relaxer gone awry, and that proteins treatment will save my hair! Although I have done several protein treatments and deep conditioners I am still noticing far more breakage than I would like to see. At this point what would you recommend that would be more beneficial for me?

A: Changing chemicals is a serious problem. Under no circumstance would I EVER do what you have done. I know very high profiled, book-writing hairdressers say it is okay to change from "no lye" to "lye" relaxers but I contend they are as wrong as two left shoes! You need to stick with what you have done now and try not to change back as you could go bald!

CR

SISTER TALK - "CHANGING TEXTURIZER TO RELAXER"

Q: Is going to a straight perm instead of the texturized perm virtually impossible?"

A: Going from a texturizer (a perm which is done with a totally different chemical) to a relaxer is out of the question unless you want to start growing your complete head of hair all over again. That is one of the biggest mistakes Sisters make with chemicals.

Some boast they did it but MOST of us cannot because it destroys the hair bonds in the hair. The hair in some cases will dissolve right on your head! Do not make this mistake.

∞

SISTER TALK - "SHOULD I DO 'LYE' OR 'NO LYE'?"

Q: My mother is an ethnic mix (her mom is half White and Native American and her dad is Black), but my Father is Black so I have mostly African-American hair features including Black kinky hair. So, what is the best relaxer to use, 'lye' or 'no lye' relaxer? I went on the Internet and found this board on Black hair and they discuss what they think are good relaxer. Right now I'm just so confused.

A: Which relaxer to use, "Lye" or "No lye?" I have come to the conclusion that one is NOT better than the other. They will both make you baldheaded IF they are misapplied and constantly applied to the scalp! So as far as which relaxer to pick, YOU MAKE THE CALL. Just ensure it is kept off your scalp! And use the same product consistently. Do not experiment!

∞

SISTER TALK - "CAN I SWITCH BACK TO 'NO LYE'?"

Q: I have a very sensitive scalp. The past two relaxers were 'lye' and I burned really bad (even when my scalp was based the second time.) Is it safe to switch back to 'no lye?' Women on an Internet hair board claim that they have experienced hair breakage due to using 'no lye' relaxers and most prefer using 'lye' relaxers. Is it true that 'no lye' relaxers can cause breakage?

A: The "Lye" or "no lye" component of a relaxer is not an indication of whether or not the relaxer will burn your head. Burning of the head is caused by getting the product on your scalp. Likewise, is it not an indication of whether or not you will have more breakage when you choose one relaxer over the other. They both cause breakage if used inappropriately and when the hair is left unmaintained. They both are caustic and will burn if they are misapplied.

To evaluate what causes our hair problems, I conducted a survey on my website of willing participants to see what Sisters were using regarding chemicals when their hair was thinning. (Results of the survey can be found at the end of this book.) The participants used either "lye" or "no lye" formulas with similar results. So it is a fallacy to suggest one is better than the other. The bottom line is that they both contain "lye" and "lye" can cause severe hair and scalp damage, breakage and burns!

∞

SISTER TALK - "SCALP BURNING WITH CHEMICALS"

Q: My problem always starts when I go to the hairdressers. I never have the same person applying my relaxer, they overprocess and they frequently do not use neutralizer! If the hairdresser does communicate with me, I always ask the same question but I seldom have questions answered satisfactorily and, frankly, what I hear sometimes just begs belief.

I have finally found a hairdresser I can trust. For how long I don't know - they start off good, but when the money starts rolling in, I notice cutbacks in the quality of products and a lapse in the service they provide. I only use the hairdressers when I need a relaxer. My friend recommended a professional product she applied it at home. She purchased it from the hairdresser!! She said it burnt like crazy! I asked her whether she applied the protective product they specify you should use and she said she used the scalp protector. I asked her whether she irritated her scalp before the relaxer was applied, and she said no. She wants to know why her scalp burnt so much and whether there is a relaxer that does not burn. Please can you advise?

A: Scalp burning can be caused by a number of reasons:

If she washed her hair less than 24-48 hours before the chemical application

If she scratched her itchy scalp a few days before the relaxer retouch

Getting relaxers on the scalp, which obviously she did

Self analysis is the key. Avoid these things in the future. And to my knowledge, there is no relaxer product on the market that will not cause burning. If used improperly, any chemical relaxer will burn.

☙

SISTER TALK - "MY FIRST RELAXER BROKE MY HAIR AND NOW I AM BALD"

Q: When I first had my hair relaxed it broke off on the left back side and continued up the side of my head past my ear. I had very thick coarse dry hair and my old stylist kept putting more grease on my scalp and advised me to do the same. After I developed bald places I went online and found your website, thank God! You are a Godsend! Thank you so much for your research and for writing your books. I realize that I have to be patient and give my hair the time it needs to grow, but it is really hard to find someone competent enough to professionally relax my hair. When I was pregnant my hair was long, healthy and beautiful. I just want it that way again. Is it possible?

A: The problem you have experienced is a sad, sad thing as it is lack of knowledge that has caused you irreversible hair damage. The hair that is gone is gone forever! You have unfortunately changed the cells under the scalp and it is almost certain if you have no hair their now, you will not have hair there in the future. Also since you have this problem, it would be very unwise to continue relaxing your hair unless you want to go completely bald!

☙

SISTER TALK - "CAN I PUT RELAXER ALL OVER MY HAIR AGAIN?"

Q: My hair has really grown and it is beginning to get unmanageable. In some spots it looks like my hair has never even been relaxed and seems to have regained too much curl. Do you think it would be a bad idea to put relaxer all over my hair again, or should I just get a retouch like I usually do?

A: The decision to re-relax your entire head of hair is your decision. However, I will tell you that if you decide to do so you better have at least three Aphogee protein treatments BEFORE proceeding so you can ensure the hair is strengthened as much as possible.

☙

SISTER TALK - "SHOULD I DO A PROTEIN TREATMENT BEFORE I RELAX?"

Q: My breakage has reduced drastically since I started using UBH products and I'm going for a retouch next month. Is it okay to use Aphogee Protein treatment on my hair before I go for my retouch just to make my hair stronger, even though I don't have severe breakage? I recently moved here and this is the first time I'm going to have my hair professionally relaxed. Would you give me brief directions on how hairdressers are supposed to relax my hair? Since I haven't been to a salon here, if they are doing something wrong I want to be able to speak up.

A: My suggestion is to do an Aphogee before having your retouch. This will strengthen your hair to provide the hair with extra reinforcement. Also be aware that most hairdressers smooth the product with the back of their hands. This is a serious flaw in technique because too much gets on the scalp. They are trained to do it this way. The consequences are dire, as it can penetrate the scalp and result in hair loss. If you choose to relax your hair this is the risk you take unless you find someone who will respect your wishes. Telling the hairdresser they are doing something wrong is "speculative." You cannot win if they are not open to suggestions. Discuss your concerns with the hairdresser BEFORE you sit down in the chair.

CR

SISTER TALK - "DO I NEED TO BASE MY SCALP?"

Q: Do you put some kind of base on your scalp before you put the perm in? I know you said to keep it off of your scalp, but I was wondering how to do it because it seems almost impossible.

A: According to the cosmetology teaching guide, there are two formulas when using relaxers: "lye" and "no lye." The "lye" formulas recommend basing the scalp and the already processed hair to avert over-processing and breaking. According to the teaching guide, the "no lye" formulas, which are more commonly used today, don't require basing.

CR

SISTER TALK - "IS VASELINE A GOOD BASE PROTECTOR?"

Q: Is it okay to use petroleum jelly as a base protector on my scalp when relaxing hair to prevent burning of the perm? I know relaxers should not be put on the scalp, but just in case some relaxer does get on the scalp would this offer protection?

A: Relaxers that you use at home are generally "no lye" or no base products. In my 35 years of relaxing my hair, I never based my scalp. When I used relaxers early on, there was a product that was included as one of the steps to put on the hair that was already relaxed. After the sticky mixture was applied and if it was allowed to dry, it made the hair quite hard like some sort of protein. Petroleum coats things just like liquid saran wrap so it may provide minimal protection. Use it if you feel it will benefit you however, it is not absolute protection against burns when the chemical is allowed to touch the scalp.

ঙ

SISTER TALK - "IS MY HAIRDRESSER WRONG?"

Q: When you do a 'touch-up', are you supposed to apply the relaxer to the new growth/roots only and that's it? The stylist I go to does root to tip.

A: Yes, you are correct. The retouch should be just on the new growth. Relaxers destroy the hair so it is important to minimize unnecessary chemical applications. Putting the chemical all over the hair every time is setting you up for failure!! When the hair is very strong my experience has been that it can be carefully done once a year without over processing the hair.

ঙ

SISTER TALK - "ARE PROTEIN TREATMENTS GOOD BEFORE OR AFTER RELAXING?"

Q: After the relaxer, you suggest having a protein treatment. If I was to use a protein treatment or UBH conditioner afterwards, wouldn't that burn if I have chemical burns from the relaxer? I'm afraid. Can you please advise?

A: Even if you don't have chemical burns, your scalp pores are wide open after a relaxer and therefore, more vulnerable. Everybody is different so to say that UBH conditioner may be rather intense on your scalp after a relaxer treatment depends on the person. I did experienced frequent burns with protein treatments after a relaxer, when I used to relax my hair. It is a tough call. To be on the safe side, if you get the chemical on your scalp at all avoid the protein treatment altogether! On the other hand, if you do the protein treatment about three days before the relaxer, you will not have that to worry about.

✿

SISTER TALK - "CAN I REAPPLY A RELAXER?"

Q: My sister went to a new stylist who uses the Affirm system and her hair is doing really great. I decided to use the same person and now my hair is a mess. The relaxer did not straighten my hair and I have major frizzes on the ends. She wants me to come back in a week so that she can relax it again, but I am afraid that my hair will fall off my head from over treatment. What do you suggest that I do?

A: Under NO circumstance should your hair be RE-relaxed without doing at least three protein treatments. I would also suggest you wait about three weeks in between relaxer applications. Do an Aphogee protein treatment each week to strengthen the hair BEFORE attempting the relaxer again. Don't use UBH conditioner when you do a protein treatment because you already have enough protein. However I do recommend the UBH Lotion Creme afterwards because the oil in the product will soften your hair after the protein treatment. After this regimen, then and only then should you have the relaxer reapplied. Your hair must be strengthened before the chemical is reapplied and a good Aphogee protein treatment will provide that.

❧

SISTER TALK - "UNDERPROCESSED RELAXER.
WHAT DO I DO NOW?"

Q: Last Friday I had my new growth relaxed and realized a couple of days later that most of the roots (65%) did not relax. They are underprocessed and still quite kinky. Based on your recommendation, right after the relaxer was rinsed out of my hair I went home and did a protein treatment. My hairdresser is blaming the under-processing on the protein treatment. I have been considering switching to another relaxer, but I am unsure of whether it would be too dangerous to reprocess the underprocessed roots. When is it safe to re-relax the under processed roots?

A: Hairdressers are notorious for blaming clients for issues they cause. I have had numerous protein treatments within minutes after having a retouch when I relaxed my hair and it NEVER affected the texture of my hair when it was freshly relaxed. I too, have had experiences where the chemical was applied wrong and it did not straighten as expected. To correct the problem this is what I recommend:

1. Do a minimum of three protein treatments before having your hair retouched.

2. Have the retouch done again in three weeks.

3. Changing a chemical is not recommended so stick with the one you are currently using until you are certain your hair is in its best condition.

58

✿

SISTER TALK - "RETOUCH OR NOT RETOUCH?"

Q: I had a relaxer about 5 weeks ago. I have not gone to the hairdresser since I received your book and products about three weeks ago. I've been doing my own hair according to your instructions. My hair looks healthy. Now my new growth is starting to come in. Is a retouch absolutely necessary to keep Black hair straight? Or should I continue to condition and moisturize it to keep it strong and soft?

A: To keep afro-textured hair permanently straight, you will have to perform retouches. Temporary straightening can be done with a flat iron. NEVER use a pressing comb on chemically processed hair. And you should continue to moisturize and condition even if you never retouch ever again.

✿

SISTER TALK - "MY RELAXER DID NOT TAKE"

Q: I put a relaxer in my hair about two weeks ago and it did not take. I was wondering if I can do another relaxer in two more weeks. I have so much new growth in the back that I can't comb my hair without it breaking. If not, what do you recommend?

A: Most relaxers must be stirred with an activator to make them work. If improperly stirred, it will not activate to straighten the hair. The new growth may look okay initially but within days it is evident it is still too coily or underprocessed. This can also happen along the hair shaft when you find those wavy sections of hair in several places throughout your hair. This happens especially if you self-relax your hair, or extend your retouch beyond 3-4 months. In most cases the wavy sections along the hair shaft are nothing more than sections that were missed because you were not able to see all over the head when the relaxer was applied. This is another reason why it is better to have someone else do your chemical treatments because they can see all over your head.

To correct this with your next retouch this is what I recommend:

1. Do a minimum of three protein treatments before having your next retouch to strengthen your hair.

2. Wait three weeks to reprocess the hair.

3. Apply the relaxer to the new growth first all around the head and properly smooth it off the scalp. If there are sections in the middle of the hair shaft that are crinkly, smooth the relaxer down the hair shaft in that area only during the last five minutes of treatment.

CR

SISTER TALK - "CAN I DO THE CORRECTIVE RELAXER PROCESS?"

Q: I have a question about the 'corrective relaxer process.' You mention in your book that sometimes you may have to do this once or twice a year. I think my hair needs this because even after I get a touch-up on just the new growth, there are several sections right in the middle layer of my hair strands that are wavy. When I get my next touch-up (which will be tomorrow,) should I put the relaxer on the new growth first and then after finishing all the new growth go back and apply relaxer to the middle layers? Also should I comb the relaxer through on the new growth only or also the middle wavy sections?

A: See the previous answer.

CR

SISTER TALK - "IS IT OKAY TO CHANGE FROM ADULT PERM TO KIDDY PERM?"

Q: I read in you book that you do not recommend switching from one perm to another. But you also stated that all perms have basically the same ingredients. If all perms have the same ingredients why is there breaking or damage when you switch from an "adult perm" to a 'kiddy perm?' If they all give the same results, why does it matter which name brand you use? So are you saying it's ok to switch as long as the chemicals and ingredients are exactly the same?

A: First I must advise you that "Adult" relaxers and "Kiddy" relaxers (aka Kiddy Perms) are only different in who they are marketed to. Adult relaxers are marketed to Black women with afro-textured hair. "Kiddy Perms" are marketed to the mothers of Black children with afro-textured hair. Put them side by side and look at the ingredients. You will see that they are exactly the same ingredients. So don't believe you are using something milder when you use a "Kiddy perm" because it is NOT. It is a marketing ploy, an adult product with a child's picture on the box to make you think it is formulated differently. Don't believe the HYPE!

The reason changing products is not advised is because different products do not always work together. One relaxer may have more of an ingredient than another; or another relaxer may require an additional chemical to counter something else. The first chemical has already restructured the hair so when the second chemical is applied, the hair may become very weak and break. Even the use of "no lye" and "lye" based products within the same product line can result in risk. It is the mixing of different chemicals that you need to be concerned about.

61

Also there is no way you can tell if the balance of ingredients are exactly the same unless you analyze each of the product's ingredients. Putting the box side by side is only an indication of what the ingredients are, but this does not offer exact measurements.

CR

SISTER TALK - "IS IT OKAY TO CHANGE RELAXERS AGAIN?"

Q: I have been using UBH products since the beginning of this year and I am seeing excellent results. I use children's relaxer in my hair right now, and they usually last me for about 3-1/2 to 4 months, but I have read the good testimonies about another relaxer. I was thinking about switching. In the past I tried others that did pretty good, but most were a little to strong for my hair. I find that the children's worked better. I would like to try another relaxer I have heard about. Would it be better for me to just stick with the children's relaxer?

A: If you have experienced problems in the past let that be your guide, not someone else's experiences!

CR

SISTER TALK - "SHEDDING TOO MUCH HAIR"

Q: I have used regular strength relaxers for many years. Over the past year or so, I have noticed my hair is shedding more than usual. When expressing concern to my hairdresser, she seemed at a loss to offer any advice. I was told this could be due to approaching menopause and that I should consider getting a weave! Needless to say, I was devastated. Would I be fighting a losing battle if I tried to get my hair to stop shedding? I wondered if I decide to keep my perm, can I switch to another brand without causing damage to my hair? I would like to grow out the perm but I don't like my hair kinky and it appears hot pressing the hair is not a viable alternative either. I also use a semi-permanent dye (no peroxide or ammonia) to cover the gray.

A: Your hair problems may or may not be related to menopause (hormones). That is the simplest answer in my opinion when no consideration is given to how the hair is being treated. I recommend you read my *Ultra Black Hair Growth II* book first because I believe you need to understand the difference between shedding and breaking as well as gain knowledge about Black hair care basics. Statistically, the odds suggest the probability of hair breakage as opposed to shedding. Do not switch chemicals. Stick with the product you are using now. Based on your email, giving up relaxing is out of the question. Also, after using UBH products you may be able to extend your relaxer. This can help you avoid applying the chemical too often, which enhances the health of the hair.

ℭℜ

SISTER TALK - "CAN I CHANGE MY CURL TO A RELAXER?"

Q: I have been using your conditioner and I have read your Ultra Black Hair book and my hair is growing like a weed! I am concerned because I have been using a curl perm for the past few years and I heard that they might be pulling this product from the shelves. It seems curly perms are being phased out. I wouldn't mind switching to a relaxer, but I read in your book that this is a BIG no-no. What's a girl to do?

A: I have no knowledge of "curl perms" being discontinued so I cannot address that topic. As far as if you can change your curl to a relaxer now, you have two choices:

1. Let your hair grow out with the curl perm on it and THEN have a relaxer. The hair that has the curl perm on it will not survive the relaxer because they are two different chemicals. Relaxers and perm products do not mix! Putting the relaxer over the permed hair will destroy the hair and cause it to fall off your head.

2. Or cut your hair off to the new growth THEN relax it.

☙

SISTER TALK - "NEW GROWTH AND THE PRESSING COMB"

Q: Because of a chemical switch, my hair is breaking badly! I really don't want to use chemicals again until my hair stops breaking. In the mean while I have to do something to the new growth. My questions are; if I wait another couple of months and go back to my original relaxer, will this be ok? I also would like to know if it is ok to use an electric hot comb on my hair since my hair is so short in spots and it is impossible to straighten it with an electric curler or flat iron.

A: Some sisters have been able to go back to their previous relaxer and others have lost their hair trying. You cannot put a hot comb or pressing comb on new growth when you relax your hair, not even the plug in type. Use a blow-dryer on the roots and flat iron if it bothers you too much. I would not do that too often either. Try sitting under the hooded dryer with UBH Lotion Creme on your hair and smooth with your hands as it is drying. That helps smooth the cuticle but it may not work for everyone. This technique works best when your hair still has a lot of the chemical on the hair. With 3"-4" of new growth you may want to section the hair, plait it and let it dry. After it dries, take the hair down and flat iron. This will help to extend your retouch. For the small pieces that are next to impossible to "pick up," I would opt for covering the spots with other hair if that is possible until it is about 1"-2", then you can straighten or curl with a small barrel curling iron.

❧

SISTER TALK - "HOW DO I USE A RELAXER?"

Q: I am writing you from Iraq and your products are truly wonderful! My favorite is the conditioner. I would like to know exactly how to use a relaxer.

A: My Sister PLEASE do not attempt to apply a relaxer if you have never used them before!

❧

SISTER TALK - "FROM ONE BRAND TO ANOTHER"

Q: My stylist wants to switch relaxers. Do you recommend that?

A: If your hairdresser makes this switch, you had better make sure your hair is strong and in good, healthy condition. Most people can't change chemicals successfully without experiencing a tremendous amount of breaking. I say stick with what you have now or change at your own risk. Or you can wait about 3-4 months until you have had time to make your hair stronger with protein treatments. Changing chemicals is very risky and can cause tremendous hair loss.

❧

SISTER TALK - "RELAXERS, OH MY!"

Q: I am 20 years old and from Antigua. Thank God I found your website. I was searching for solutions to the problem that we Black women have with our hair and came across your site. The first time I saw it, I was hooked and I am on it everyday. Your site is informative and based on common sense. I never knew how important moisture was to our hair and that switching relaxers is bad until I read your tips, some of which I've applied and have seen some results. Now I want to order your book and products.

I used one relaxer for my last retouch but I used to use another one regularly before. I was wondering if I should continue using the one I have on my hair now or switch back to the previous relaxer? A hairdresser told me that one particular brand may result in thinning and that another will work well with my hair. That's why I switched. I know my hair was breaking before but it was because of the regular blow drying and I don't think that the first relaxer was responsible. So can I switch back to previous relaxer?

A: Your hairdresser is wrong! There is no proven evidence that one particular relaxer thins the hair. They ALL will thin the hair if they are misapplied. If the chemical is pushed onto the scalp when applied, ANY relaxer will thin the hair. Do not keep switching back and forth with chemicals. Stick with the one you are currently using to avoid destroying your hair.

ℭℛ

SISTER TALK - "FROM RELAXED HAIR TO TEXTURIZED HAIR"

Q: I stumbled on your website trying to find information on texturizing. Presently my hair is relaxed and I would like to switch to wearing my hair texturized for a while. My hair is about 3" long. My stylist says that I would have to cut my hair down to the new growth to do this. I have less than a half inch of new growth and I do not want to go that short. I know that I will have to cut it shorter but, do I really have to cut my hair that much shorter to texturize it or can this same texturized look be achieved by simply applying relaxer and washing it out before it becomes straight?

A: Your stylist is correct in that the hair would need to be cut down to the new growth. Putting a texturizer over a relaxer is a BIG mistake and will destroy your hair. Relaxers and texturizers contain two different chemicals. Some individuals have used "relaxer products to texturize" by putting the chemical on for a shorter time period and not allowing it to completely straighten the hair. Most people with afro-textured hair will not find this look suitable because the hair will not produce the wavy curls expected because afro-textured hair is coily. Loosening the coil will not convert the hair to waves! The results are a knotty looking, partially relaxed coil. Waves for afro-textured hair must be produced on a "perm rod" to get the effect of "waves and curls."

CR

SISTER TALK - "MY HAIRDRESSER CHANGED MY CHEMICAL!"

Q: I started using your product in April of this year. All was going well until about a month ago. My hair was growing slow, but steady. About a month ago my hair started coming out in long strands when I combed it. I thought it was because I needed a touch up. It had been eight weeks since my last touch up. Now that I have had my touch up it seems to be getting worse! So why would my hair start doing this all of a sudden? I use to just have a problem with breakage. Now it's not breaking but coming out in strands when I comb it. I'm using a wide tooth comb, what else can I do? At this rate I'll be bald in three months. I spoke with my hairdresser and she confirmed she changed my relaxer, which you say is a big problem. Do I go back to my old relaxer the next time or do I keep using the one that she used?

A: What do you do now? Fire your hairdresser! The faulty practice of hairdressers is one of the reasons we suffer hair loss.

Is there hope for your hair now? Only if the hair has not been destroyed, which can often happen when you mix chemicals. The only thing you can do is apply protein treatments and hope it helps. You can also file a lawsuit on her for malpractice. (A bit extreme but true.) Can you go back to the other chemical? NO! Doing that will only intensify your problems. The resulting scenario will be one chemical mixed with the one you have now and one more chemical mixed with the already messed up mess. Sadly, there is no correction for hairdresser stupidity!

7. UBH Thinning Hair Survey Results

review our 2006 survey

Q1

Are you male or female?

Male..............10..........0.62%

Female.....1598........99.38%

Total   1608

Q2

Are you experiencing thinning hair?

No ....257.....16.29%

Yes................1321.....83.71%

Total   1578

Q3

What race are you?

Black or African American (Not Hispanic or Latino)	1213	92.38%
Black or African American and White (Not Hispanic or Latino)	32	2.44%
Black and Asian (Chinese, Filipano, Japanese, Korean, Vietnamese)	2	0.15%
Black and American Indian	46	3.50%
Black and Other Pacific Islander (Native Hawaiian, Guamanian or Samoan	3	0.23%
Black and Hispanic (Mexican, Puerto Rican, Cuban)	14	1.07%
Hispanic or Latino	2	0.15%
White	1	0.08%
Total	**1313**	

Q4

How long have you experienced thinning hair problems?
(How long has the hair been gone?)

1-6 months	250	19.64%
7-12 months	175	13.75%
1-3 years	434	34.09%
4-10 year	281	22.07%
11-20 years	82	6.44%
20+ years	51	4.01%
Total	**1273**	

Q5

Where is the hair thinning?

On the top (front) of the head	139	10.61%
Crown (middle) of the head	198	15.11%
Around the sides, edges or temples	380	29.01%
Back of head or neckline	112	8.55%
Crown (middle) and back of head	47	3.59%
Crown (middle) and sides, edges or temples	112	8.55%
Entire head (thinning all over)	228	17.40%
Other	94	7.18%
Total	**1310**	

Q6

Do you have any of these issues?

Severe internal issues	17	1.36%
Medical issues (thyroid, chemo therapy etc)	79	6.30%
Don't Know	195	15.56%
None of the above	962	76.78%
Total	**1253**	

Q7

Do you braid your hair with hair extensions?

Yes	413	33.17%
No	832	66.83%
Total	**1245**	

Q8

Do you wear hair weaves? (Select all that apply)

Braided/Track/Cornrow Weave (Sew-in weave)	235	18.86%
Net Weave		
(Cap/net weave with other hair attached to it)	24	1.93%
Bonded (Glued on Weave)	70	5.62%
Infusion (Hot glue and hot glue gun)	2	0.16%
Clip-on Weave	57	4.57%
I don't wear weaves	763	61.24%
Other	95	7.62%
Total	**1246**	

Q9

Do you wear press and curl?

Yes	194	15.73%
No	1039	84.27%

Total 1233

Q10

Do you use heated appliances to style your hair?

No	398	32.31%
Yes	834	67.69%

Total   1232

Q11

Which heated appliances do you use? (Select all that apply)

Blowdryer	588	25.18%
Curling Iron (plug in)	556	23.81%
Curling Iron (heated on a stove)	121	5.18%
Flat Iron (plut in)	386	16.53%
Flat Iron (heated on a stove)	62	2.66%
Hooded or Dome type dryer	453	19.40%
Pressing comb (plug in)	71	3.04%
Pressing comb (heated on a stove)	98	4.20%
Total	**2335**	

Q12

Which answer best describes your hairs current state?

Natural (No chemicals for 1+ years)	236	19.22%
Relaxed (Straight perm)	934	76.06%
Permed (Curly perm or Texturizer)	58	4.72%
Total	**1228**	

Q13

Which chemical relaxer do you use?

Lye	249	26.86%
No Lye	678	73.14%
Total	**927**	

Q14

Who performs your chemical process? (Straight perm or Curly perm)

I apply them myself	327	33.30%
I have a friend or family member apply them for me	126	12.83%
I have my hair professionally processed with chemicals	529	53.87%
Total	**982**	

Q15

How much time do you allow between your chemicals before they are retouched?

2 - 4 weeks	20	2.04%
4 - 6 weeks	265	27.01%
6 - 8 weeks	379	38.63%

8 - 10 weeks	156	15.90%
10 - 12 weeks	70	7.14%
12 + weeks	91	9.28%
Total	**981**	

Q16

How long have you relaxed/chemically processed your hair?
(Straight perm or Curly perm)

1-3 years	124	12.70%
4-6 years	72	7.38%
7-10 years	141	14.45%
11-20 years	334	34.22%
20+ years	305	31.25%
Total	**976**	

Q17

Did you use chemicals on your hair in the past and have
stopped using chemicals?

I have never used chemicals on my hair	31	2.57%
No, I still use chemicals on my hair	803	66.58%
Yes, I have stopped using chemicals on my hair	372	30.85%
Total	**1206**	

Q18

If you no longer use chemicals, when was your last chemical treatment (relaxer or perm) applied?

6 months to 1 year	139	36.20%
1 - 3 years	85	22.14%
3 - 5 years	34	8.85%
5 - 10 years	40	10.42%
10 - 20 years	12	3.13%
20 + years	3	0.78%
Other	71	18.49%
Total	**384**	

Q19

Has a medical doctor diagnosed your thinning hair problem?

No	1084	90.11%
Yes	119	9.89%
Total	**1203**	

Q20

What was the medical doctors diagnosis of your thinning hair?

Androgenetic Alopecia (usually inherited, characteristic of male pattern baldness)	13	10.48%
Alopecia Areata (sudden hair loss or irregular patterns)	21	16.94%
Telogen Effluvium (shock, trauma, drug intake, fever)	5	4.03%
Traction or Traumatic Alopecia (repetitive pulling or twisting, excessive chemical use, hot comb use)	20	16.13%
Postpartum Alopecia (after pregnancy)	3	2.42%
I don't recall what it is called	17	13.71%
Other	45	36.29%
Total	**124**	

Q21

Do you use hair color?

Yes	468	38.90%
No	735	61.10%
Total	**1203**	

Q22

What type of hair color do you use?

Permanent color	169	36.19%
Semi-Permanent color or a Rinse	298	63.81%
Total	**467**	

Q23

Which answer best describes your balding/thinning condition?

Bald spots and patches	442	37.05%
Fuzzy (baby hair)	731	61.27%
Completely Bald	20	1.68%
Total	**1193**	

Q24

Education level

Not High School Graduate	46	3.89%
High School Graduate (including equivalency)	169	14.27%
Some college or associate degree	533	45.02%
Bachelors Degree	307	25.93%
Masters Degree	102	8.61%
Doctoral degree or professional degree	27	2.28%
Total	**1184**	

Q25

Age group

16 - 20 years	88	7.45%
21 - 29 years	244	20.66%
30 - 39 years	357	30.23%
40 - 49 years	311	26.33%
50 - 59 years	153	12.96%
60 + years	28	2.37%
Total	**1181**	

Bibliography

A'Lelia Bundles, <u>On Her Own Ground - The Life and Times of Madam C.J. Walker</u> (New York: Scribner, 2001), p. 68

<u>American Heritage College Dictionary,</u> "Sodium Hydroxide"

"Androgenetic Alopecia -The Adverse Effect of DHT", accessed 27 Nov 2004; available from www.hairprime.com; Internet.

Avre Cosmetic Ingredients Dictionary, accessed 18 April 2006; available from www.avreskincare.com; Internet.

Ayana D. Byrd & Lori L. Tharps, <u>Hair Story, Untangling the Roots of Black Hair in America</u> (New York: St. Martin's Griffin, 2001), p. 88.

"Causes of Thinning Hair", accessed 26 Mar 2006; available from www.hairprime.com; Internet.

"Guide to Inspections of Cosmetic Product Manufacturers", accessed 25 April 2006; available from www.fda.gov; Internet.

Milady's Standard Textbook of Cosmetology, (New York: 2000), p. 65-66, p. 367, p. 372-373.

Nekhena Evans, <u>Hairlocking Everything You need to Know</u> (Brookyn, NY: A&B Publishers Group, 2004), p. 53.

"Room to Grow: The Ethnic Hair Care Industry has potential, but growth is still slow", accessed 30 April 2006; available from www.Happi.com; Internet

CATHY HOWSE
A PIONEER IN THE HAIR CARE INDUSTRY

Determination, drive and commitment are what make Cathy Howse a dynamo in the hair care industry. Being a single mother of two was never a deterrent to reaching her goals. Despite the odds, she became the only child out of 7 to graduate from college. Cathy used her degree in Industrial Marketing in the software industry before deciding to take her knowledge and start her own company.

Cathy's vision was to change the world of hair care for Black women. She set out to challenge the traditional methods Black women used and replace them with an educated approach to caring for their hair. She made it her purpose to empower others and help them realize the truths about Black hair and as a result experience better, healthier hair.

After years of research, Cathy decided to put her findings in a book. In 1989, she published *Ultra Black Hair Growth*, which she updated in 1994 and again in 2000. Her research had not only delivered educational information for her book but some scientific data as well; so in 1992, Cathy developed her own conditioner-and in 1997, she developed a dew spray moisturizer. Before long, her products were in demand around the world and thousands of Black women were achieving long, healthy hair.

Yet, Cathy believes it was the launch of the website ultrablackhair.com that took her company to the next level. Her sales increased and she added three staff members. Her vision had been realized and the company she started on a shoestring was now a household name.

The hair care industry recognizes her as the author of the only proven black hair growth process in the world. Her books *Ultra Black Hair Growth and* its updated versions, *Ultra Black Hair Growth II* and *Ultra Black Hair Growth 2000* have sold more than 100,000 copies. Her newest book, the long-awaited *Thinning Edges: A Chemical Reaction,* is sure to share in that success.

Cathy's biography appears in Who's Who in America, Who's Who of American Women and Who's Who in the World.

Cathy's Product Picks

UBH Spray Moisturizer

Available in 8, 16 and 32 ounce sizes

It's Soft!

Dew is a moisturizer that's used daily to soften and replace lost moisture in dry hair. Use it as a light conditioner when you want a smooth, chic texture that bounces. Great for natural or chemically processed hair.

It's Light!

Dew is a refreshing break from heavy moisturizers and conditioners. Use Dew when you twist, lock, perm, relax or color-treat. Dew's light non-greasy formula moisturizes, conditions and adds shine.

It's You!

For sensational hair! Bouncy Hair! Silky, healthy hair!

Cathy's Product Picks

UBH Lotion Creme Moisturizer

Available in 8, 16 and 32 ounce sizes

Soften

Lotion is a creme moisturizer that's used daily to soften and replace lost moisture in dry hair. Use after a protein treatment to soften or after a deep condition. Softens hair to minimize breakage.

Smooth

Lotion imparts light oil to smooth dry hair types when natural or when you extend a chemical retouch. Penetrating formula gets to the source of dry hair.

Experience

Soft, shiny hair. Non-greasy, sensational hair!

Cathy's Product Picks

UBH Conditioner

Available in 8, 16 and 32 ounce sizes

Strengthen!

Ultra Black Hair conditioner provides protein to regularly strengthen a dry hair type to stop brittle hair that breaks. Used as a deep conditioning treatment it actually improves a dry hair condition. Just enough protein to attach itself to the hair strengthening it to stop breakage.

Lubricate!

Dry hair needs external oil to lubricate the inner most part of your hair to soften dry brittle hair.

Stimulate!

Stimulate the hair cells underneath the scalp without damaging hair brushes. Increase blood circulation to stimulate hair cell production.

Toll Free Orders 1-800-754-8751 • www.ultrablackhair.com